Sayings
for
Leaders

David C. Jones, editor

DETSELIG
ENTERPRISES LTD

* 2003 David C. Jones

National Library of Canada Cataloguing in Publication Data

Main entry under title:

Sayings for leaders/David C. Jones, editor

ISBN 1-55059-259-9

1. Leadership--Quotations, maxims, etc. I. Jones, David C.
PN6084.L15S29   2003   158'.4   C2003-911089-3

210-1220 Kensington Rd. N.W., Calgary, AB T2N 3P5

Phone: 403-283-0900/Fax: 403-283-6947

DETSELIG Email: temeron@telusplanet.net
ENTERPRISES LTD

www.temerondetselig.com

We acknowledge the financial support of the Government of Canada through the Book Publishing Industry Development Program (BPIDP) and the Alberta Foundation for the Arts for our publishing activities.

The Alberta Foundation for the Arts Alberta
COMMITTED TO THE DEVELOPMENT OF CULTURE AND THE ARTS

ISBN 1-55059-259-9

SAN 115-0324

Printed in Canada

Dedication

To Paramahansa Yogananda
& J. Donald Walters,
teachers

Note from the Editor

I have altered the gender of some quotations to provide balance. Such quotations are credited with the phrase, "adapted from."

These publishers or rights holders have granted permission to use quotations: the Krishnamurti Foundation of America, Ojai, California, for J. Krishnamurti, *Think on These Things* (1970) and *Beyond Violence* (1973); Penguin Putnam, New York, for Neale Walsch, *Conversations with God, Book 1* (1996), and *Conversations with God, Book 3*; Foundation for *A Course in Miracles* (1975), Temecula, California; Crystal Clarity Publishers (www.cystalclarity.com, phone: 800-424-1055) for J. Donald Walters, *Secrets of Life* (1992, 1993, 1994), *Do It Now!* (1995), and *Little Secrets of Success* (1994).

Introduction

Everyone is a leader, whether timid or triumphant, with few followers or many. And every leader creates the self that leads, a self of minute constriction or infinite possibility, a wisp or a mountain. Some selves are artistic creations, utterly compelling – a tapestry of golden intentions and honest deliberations, for instance, or an individual expression of kindness and consideration, or a beacon that guides the inexperienced through the reefs of grievance and greed. Some selves are a comfort, a support, an example.

Whenever a creator chooses such artistry, he cultivates an inner seed that has always been with him. Put another way, he chooses to become what he always was, and he accepts what he *is*. And in that sacred moment of acceptance, he emanates the harmony that is the spirit of a natural leader.

As the leader sees herself, so will she see others. She cannot love herself more than she respects others, because she cannot love herself *if* she disrespects them. Who can embrace herself who has degraded and diminished another? For the ensuing guilt is a form of self-regret, self-disappointment, and at its worst, self-loathing, and we can scarcely love what we loathe, even if it be ourselves.

Is the natural leader a reformer? Yes, potentially of the

whole world – but of herself *first*, then of willing others, by the attractiveness of her personality and radiance.

Such radiance is inherently uplifting, thus all genuine leadership is supportive. And support implies trust – any leadership that does not trust its followers, its colleagues, is *not* supportive in the most fundamental way, because mistrust always undermines, and *never* supports. "Trusting your brothers," says *A Course in Miracles*, "is essential to establishing and holding up your faith in your ability to transcend doubt and lack of sure conviction in yourself." (workbook, 329) Failure to trust subordinates will sap your faith in yourself. If they cannot be counted on, you will doubt them, and if you doubt them you can never be sure about *yourself*, for they will always seem to subvert, misunderstand or distort your intentions and leave you in chaos. And what is chaos but complete uncertainty, wherein nothing can be trusted, including yourself?

Trust is the bedrock on which the whole process of self-realization stands. Can you crystallize your highest ideals, can you manifest them? Can your prayers be answered, can you find inner wisdom? Can you inspire others to do these things? Each step requires trust, first of yourself, then of others. But fascinatingly, when the first at last comes, the second is in its train.

David C. Jones

Foundations of a Leader

A Leader's Credo

The supreme prayer of my heart is not to be learned, rich, famous, powerful or even good, but simply to be radiant. I desire to radiate health, cheerfulness, calm courage and goodwill. I wish to live without hate, whim, jealousy, envy, fear. I wish to be simple, honest, frank, natural, clean in mind and clean in body, unaffected – to say, "I do not know," if it be so, and to meet all men on an absolute equality, to face any obstacle and meet every difficulty unabashed and unafraid.

I wish others to live their lives, too, up to their highest, fullest and best. To that end I pray that I may never meddle, interfere, dictate, give advice that is not wanted, or assist when my services are not needed. If I can help people, I'll do it by giving them a chance to help themselves; and if I can uplift or inspire, let it be by example, inference and suggestion, rather than by injunction and dictation. That is to say, I desire to be Radiant – to Radiate Life!

Elbert Hubbard

Begin with yourself

You can spend an eternity looking elsewhere for truth and love, intelligence and goodwill, imploring God and man – all in vain. You must begin in yourself, with yourself – this is the inexorable law…. Leave alone the reforms and mind the reformer. You talk so much of reforms: economic, social, political. What kind of world can a man create who is stupid, greedy and heartless?

Nisargadatta Maharaj

You must be the change you wish to see in the world.

Mahatma Gandhi

Types of Leaders

An Arabian proverb says there are four sorts of people:

He who knows not and knows not he knows not: he is a fool – shun him.

She who knows not and knows she knows not: she is simple – teach her.

He who knows and knows not he knows: he is asleep – wake him.

She who knows and knows she knows: she is wise – follow her.

Adapted from Lady Isabel Burton

A Leader's Sense of Oneness

The purpose of the ancient religions of India is to plant the seeds of love in the human heart, so that they may sprout into saplings of endurance, and blossom into tolerance, yielding ultimately the fruit of peace. The pinnacle of Indian thought is non-duality, experience of the One, negation of duality. Some countries proceed towards the ideal of individual freedom, others aim at state sovereignty and the suppression of the individual's right to freedom. But Bharat has, from time immemorial, sought to infuse in the individual the conviction that he can be free only when he realizes his identity with all – not only with the inhabitants of his own state, or people who use his language or are of his own colour and creed. Expansion is the key to happiness, and love is the unfailing key to expansion.

Sathya Sai Baba

Proclaim it in any way we may, in any beautiful form, with any illustrations, if we can produce the consciousness of a Unity in all the diversity, a kinship between all animated forms, we will be bestowing on the world the greatest blessing.

N. Sri Ram

A Leader's Character

Character is the hallmark of humanity. A life without good character is a shrine without light, a coin that is counterfeit, a kite with the string broken.

Sathya Sai Baba

A Leader's Purpose

Life should be chiefly service. Without that ideal, the intelligence which God has given you is not reaching out toward its goal. When in service you forget the little self, you will feel the big Self of Spirit. As the vital rays of the sun nurture all, so should you spread rays of hope in the hearts of the poor and forsaken, kindle courage in the hearts of the despondent, and light a new strength in the hearts of those who think that they are failures.

Paramahansa Yogananda

A Leader's Faith

There is always a best and a right way to do things.

The URANTIA Book, 280

It is love alone that leads to right action. What brings order in the world is to love and let love do what it will.

J. Krishnamurti

A Leader's Role

In a government of the people, a leader should be a teacher – he should carry the torch of truth.

Robert G. Ingersoll

For in the end we will conserve only what we love, we will love only what we understand and we will understand only what we have been taught.

Baba Dioum

What do you do the best?

What gives you the greatest sense of fulfillment?

That is where your task lies.

Emmanuel

Techniques of a Leader

Acting

Everyone feels instinctively that all the beautiful sentiments in the world weigh less than a single lovely action.

Adapted from James Russell Lowell

Answering

Return calls within forty-eight hours. Never leave one unanswered.

Richard A. Moran

Anticipating

Deal with it before it happens. Set things in order before there is confusion.

Lao-tse

Apologizing

I asked Tom if countries always apologized when they had done wrong, and he says, "Yes, the little ones does."

Mark Twain

Appreciating

Would you have your name smell sweet with the myrrh of remembrance and chime melodiously in the ear of future days, then cultivate faith, not doubt, and give every man credit for the good he does, never seeking to attribute base motives to beautiful acts.

Elbert Hubbard

Beginning

When beginning an undertaking, don't ask, "What have others done before?" Ask instead, each time, "What does this particular enterprise require?"

J. Donald Walters

Bullying

Don't bully yourself. Violence will make you hard and rigid.

Nisargadatta Maharaj

Coloring

Become conscious of colors as channels of energy. Surround yourself with cheerful, harmonious colors. Inhale them mentally. Shun dark, "muddy" or depressing hues. When selecting foods, also, choose them for their diversity of colors. Color diversity in food will help ensure that your diet has the proper balance.

J. Donald Walters

Completing

Nothing is so fatiguing as the eternal hanging on of an uncompleted task.

William James

Being Consistent

This is the sin of all sins: saying one thing and acting quite the opposite, denying in practice what you assert as precept.

Sathya Sai Baba

Consorting

Cultivate an affinity with those you admire, and let that affinity span the ages and conquer time.

DCJ

Criticizing

Criticism should not be querulous and wasting, all knife and root-puller, but guiding, instructive, inspiring, a south wind, not an east wind.

Ralph Waldo Emerson

He may only chastise who loves.

Rabindranath Tagore

He can see a louse as far away as China, but is unconscious of an elephant on his nose.

Malay proverb

A drama critic is a man who leaves no turn unstoned.

George Bernard Shaw

Diversifying

Maintain outside interests. Volunteer in not-for-profits, and stay physically fit.

Richard A. Moran

Diversify not only your financial investments, as monetary counselors advise, but more importantly your investments in energy. Cultivate ever-fresh ideas, fresh interests, fresh relationships – fresh reasons, above all, for enjoying life.

J. Donald Walters

Divorcing

She cried – and the judge wiped her tears with my checkbook.

Tommy Manville

Emancipating

The butterfly flitting from flower to flower
        Ever remains mine.
I lose the one that is netted by me.

                Rabindranath Tagore

    If the world knew how to use freedom without abusing it, tyranny would not exist.

                Tehyi Hsieh

Emancipation from the bondage of the soil
        is no freedom for the tree.

                Rabindranath Tagore

Enthusing

Science may have found a cure for most evils, but it has found no remedy for the worst of them all – the apathy of human beings.

Helen Keller

It is good to be enthusiastic about a thing or two, but better if enthusiasm itself is part of what you *are* and how you greet many things. Expand your curiosity, interests and fascinations, because enthusiasm is an unfailing measure of your own self-chosen capacity for *delight*.

DCJ

Do not say, "It is morning," and dismiss it with a name of yesterday. See it for the first time as a newborn child that has no name.

Rabindranath Tagore

Nothing is interesting if you're not interested.

Helen MacInnes

Erring

Six Mistakes of Leaders

1. The delusion that personal gain is made by crushing others.

2. The tendency to worry about things that cannot be changed or corrected.

3. Insisting that a thing is impossible because we cannot accomplish it.

4. Refusing to set aside trivial preferences.

5. Neglecting development and refinement of the mind, and not acquiring the habit of reading and study.

6. Attempting to compel others to believe and live as we do.

Adapted from Cicero

Failing

A man is never so near success as when that which he calls failure has overtaken him, for it is on occasions of this sort that he is forced to THINK. If he thinks accurately and with persistence, he discovers that so-called failure is usually nothing more than a signal to rearm himself with a new plan or purpose.

Napoleon Hill

Focusing

Focus your energies, release them as a prayer, and let their innate intelligence do the work.

DCJ

Forgiving

What could you want forgiveness cannot give? Do you want peace? Forgiveness offers it. Do you want happiness, a quiet mind, a certainty of purpose, and a sense of worth and beauty that transcends the world? Do you want care and safety, and the warmth of sure protection always? Do you want a quietness that cannot be disturbed, a gentleness that never can be hurt, a deep abiding comfort, and a rest so perfect it can never be upset?

All this forgiveness offers you, and more. It sparkles on your eyes as you awake, and gives you joy with which to meet the day. It soothes your forehead while you sleep, and rests upon your eyelids so you see no dreams of fear and evil, malice and attack. And when you awake again, it offers you another day of happiness and peace. All this forgiveness offers you, and more.

A Course in Miracles, workbook, 213

Being Gentle

Cultivate a dynamic gentleness which makes others gentle.

N. Sri Ram

Being Gracious

Develop graciousness and appreciation. These are marks of a refined nature. If you cede points to others, you will win them as friends and lighten the burden of self-centeredness that is the chief obstacle to true success.

J. Donald Walters

Even hatred of vileness
Distorts a person's features.

Adapted from Bertolt Brecht

Intending

It is only by being dead earnest that one can progress quickly.

Aurobindo

The moment you are very clear about what you want to do, things happen. Life comes to your aid – a friend, a relation, a teacher, a grandmother, somebody helps you.... If you say, "This is what I really want to do and I am going to pursue it," then you will find that something miraculous takes place. You may have to go hungry, struggle to get through, but you will be a worthwhile human being, not a mere copy, and that is the miracle of it.

J. Krishnamurti

Interpreting

A fool sees not the same tree that a wise man sees.

William Blake

You can't solve a problem with a mind that created it. You have to change the mind.

Albert Einstein

Invigorating

Need and struggle are what excite and inspire us.

William James

However inspiring past victories may be, to dwell on them is to dilute energy for present challenges.

DCJ

Loving

The cure for all the ills and wrongs, the cares, the sorrows, and the crimes of humanity, all lie in the one word, "love." It is the divine vitality that everywhere produces and restores life. To each and every one of us, it gives the power of working miracles.

Lydia M. Child

Love is, ideally, the state in which the distinction between self and another has vanished. This does not mean that we abolish individuality, but we learn to regard the happiness, the progress, the interests of another as our own.

N. Sri Ram

You who were created by Love like Itself can hold no grievances and know your Self. To hold a grievance is to forget who you are.... It is as sure that those who hold grievances will suffer guilt, as it is certain that those who forgive will find peace. It is as sure that those who hold grievances will forget who they are, as it is certain that those who forgive will remember.

Grievances are completely alien to love. Grievances attack love and keep its light obscure. If I hold grievances I am attacking love, and therefore attacking my Self. My Self thus becomes alien to me.

A Course in Miracles, workbook, 114, 147

Do you know what it means to love somebody? Do you know what it means to love a tree, or a bird, or a pet animal, so that you take care of it, feed it, cherish it, though it may give you nothing in return, though it may not offer you shade, or follow you, or depend on you? Most of us don't love in that way, we don't know what that means at all because our love is always hedged about with anxiety, jealousy, fear – which implies that we depend inwardly on another, we want to be loved. We don't just love and leave it there, but we ask something in return; and in that very asking we become dependent.

So freedom and love go together. Love is not a reaction. If I love you because you love me, that is mere trade, a thing to be bought in the market; it is not love. To love is not to ask anything in return, not even to feel that you are giving something – and it is only such love that can know freedom.

J. Krishnamurti

The worst loneliness is not to be comfortable with yourself.

Mark Twain

Being Loyal

Loyalty and fidelity are not qualities for which one has to do yoga.

Aurobindo

Originating

Understand originality to be, not something that no one has ever done before, but something that originates in you. Though it has been expressed by others a thousand times, your own sincere expression of it will make it uniquely yours.

J. Donald Walters

Read something no one else is reading. Think every day something no one else is thinking. It is bad for the mind to be always part of a unanimity.

Christopher Morley

Peacemaking

Today, be a peace-maker: not in the sense of reconciling differences, but of emanating inner peace to all. Harmonize the vibrations of your heart; then expand those vibrations into your environment and into the hearts of all with whom you come in contact.

J. Donald Walters

Persevering

No difficulty can be presented to the human mind which the human mind, if it will, cannot solve. One has to be more persistent than the difficulty; there is no other way.

Aurobindo

Persuading

Leadership is the ability to decide what is to be done and to get others to want to do it.

Dwight Eisenhower

Presenting

Take a good presentation skills class.

Richard A. Moran

Quieting

To be, just *be*, is important. You need not ask anything, nor do anything. Such apparently lazy way of spending time is highly regarded in India. It means that for the time being you are free from the obsession with "what next." When you are not in a hurry and the mind is free from anxieties, it becomes quiet, and in the silence something may be heard which is ordinarily too fine and subtle for perception. The mind must be open and quiet to see. What we are trying to do here is to bring our minds into the right state for understanding what is real.

Nisargadatta Maharaj

Reconciling

He drew a circle and shut me out –
Heretic, rebel, a thing to flout.
But love and I had the wit to win:
We drew a circle and took him in!

Edwin Markham

Relaxing and Respiring

Be relaxed both physically and mentally. Tension holds illness in the body, whereas relaxation releases it and banishes it. To relax completely, first tense the body all over; then exhale forcibly and relax. Feel the tension leave your body. Mentally release all your cares and worries into the receptive vastness of space.

Enjoy being in the fresh air. Breathe more consciously. With every breath, inhale vitality and courage into your mind and body; exhale stale thoughts, discouragement and old habit patterns. Breathe in a sense of inner freedom; breathe out any sense of lingering bondage.

J. Donald Walters

Respecting

Men and women are respectable only as they respect.

Adapted from Ralph Waldo Emerson

Sacrificing

Keep in mind: It is loyalty, not sacrifice, that Jesus demands. The consciousness of sacrifice implies the absence of that wholehearted affection which would have made such a loving service a supreme joy. The idea of duty signifies that you are servant-minded and hence are missing the mighty thrill of doing your service as a friend and for a friend. The impulse of friendship transcends all convictions of duty, and the service of a friend for a friend can never be called a sacrifice.

The URANTIA Book, 1945

Selecting Leaders

A selection committee gets its own level of acuity in those it hires, a reflection of its own sensitivity, maturity, and understanding. Hence, thoughtfulness, efficiency, fairness, and kindness are necessary in the committee.

DCJ

Self-empowering

Certain mental attitudes resemble postures of the body. Do you lean forward mentally, as if to grasp things before they happen? Do you lean back, as if to distance yourself from life's unpleasantness? Do you lean sideways, as if forever seeking a new strategy? Keep your mental posture upright and relaxed, and you'll find within you the power to cope with every difficulty.

J. Donald Walters

Experience is the germ of power.

The one who is worthy of being a leader will never complain of the stupidity of helpers, the ingratitude of humankind, or the inappreciation of the public. These things are all part of the great game of life, and to meet them and not go down before them in discouragement and defeat, is the final proof of power.

Adapted from Elbert Hubbard

The moment we are aware of a hindrance in our nature to that fulfillment which all life unconsciously seeks, aware of it as a fetter upon ourselves, that moment we are on the way to its abolition.

N. Sri Ram

Speaking

The way you say a thing is part of what you say, so you have to choose the right way.

Isabel Bishop

Many argue; not many converse.

Louisa May Alcott

A favor is half granted when gracefully refused.

Publilius Syrus

Standing Here

The lesson which life repeats and constantly reinforces is "look under foot." You are always nearer the divine and the true sources of your power than you think. The lure of the distant and the difficult is deceptive. The great opportunity is where you are. Do not despise your own place and hour. Every place is under the stars, every place is the center of the world.

John Burroughs

Bloom where you're planted.

Mary Engelbreit

Suspecting

He who is too much afraid of being duped has lost the power of being magnanimous.

Henri Frederic Amiel

Thinking

Make not your thoughts your prisons.

William Shakespeare

Trouble-shooting

A small trouble is like a pebble. Hold it too close to your eye, and it fills the whole world and puts everything out of focus. Hold it at proper viewing distance, and it can be examined and properly classified. Throw it at your feet, and it can be seen in its true setting, just one more tiny bump on the pathway to eternity.

Celia Luce

Understanding

I miss the meaning of my own part
>In the play of life
Because I know not the parts
>That others play.

Rabindranath Tagore

Weeping

It is a great error to teach boys and young men that it is unmanly to show tenderness or otherwise to give evidence of emotional feeling or physical suffering. Sympathy is a worthy attribute of the male as well as the female. It is not necessary to be calloused in order to be manly. This is the wrong way to create courageous men. The world's great men have not been afraid to mourn.... Being sensitive and responsive to human need creates genuine and lasting happiness, while such kindly attitudes safeguard the soul from the destructive influences of anger, hate, and suspicion.

The URANTIA Book, 1575

Well-wishing

Goodwill is the one and only asset that competition cannot undersell nor destroy.

Marshall Field

It is impossible to feel peace unless one has positive good will towards others, not just to one's special friends and allies, and denied to others.

N. Sri Ram

The Leader As...

A Bean Sprout

A bean is pretty smart. Nature provides the bean with a quantity of nourishment to keep it going until it gets a start in life. When planted in the ground, it sends up a sprout to take a look around. There it could say, "I'll just grow in this lovely sunshine and put out a lot of leaves. I have plenty of bean meat to keep me going for a while." But the bean, being smart, does no such thing. Instead, it uses its store of nourishment to send roots deep into the earth. Only then is it ready to put out leaves in the sunshine.

Charles Kettering

A Child

Take time to listen to the children playing. From their laughter, learn lessons in innocence. From their openness, learn lessons in trust. From their guilelessness, learn lessons in truthfulness and sincerity. It isn't maturity that robs us of these virtues: It is immaturity, embittered by disappointment. With maturity comes understanding; from understanding comes acceptance; and from acceptance, finally comes wisdom.

J. Donald Walters

A Compromiser

A seeker wanted to know the difference between the master and himself.

Answered Nisargadatta Maharaj: "The common things of life: I experience them just as you do. The difference lies in what I do not experience. I do not experience fear or greed, hate or anger. I ask nothing, refuse nothing, keep nothing. In these matters I do not compromise. Maybe this is the outstanding difference between us. I will not compromise, I am true to myself, while you are afraid of reality."

A Cork

Benjamin Hoff retells the story of Confucius who stood with his disciples near the thunderous, thousand-foot waterfall at the Gorge of Lu. Down the water plunged with irresistible, deadly force, creating clouds of mist and spray.

One day, Confucius saw an old man in the pool below being tossed violently to and fro in the torrent. Immediately, Confucius rushed to save the white-haired man, but when he arrived, the gentleman was already out of danger, ashore, and singing to himself.

"No one could survive that!" Confucius exclaimed. "How did you do it?"

"Easily," the old man replied. "I learned the secret as a youngster. I go up with the waves and down with them. I move with the turbulence and never against it. I swim with the inconceivable energy of the water, and never resist it. It's quite simple, really."

A Creator

It is the creative potential itself in human beings that is the image of God.

Mary Daly

A Delayer

Nothing will ever be attempted if all possible objections must be first overcome.

Samuel Johnson

A Delegator

The wisest decision I ever made was realizing I could not do everything by myself.

J. C. Penny

A Dolt

In the Bob Hope Golf Classic... the participation of President Gerald Ford was more than enough to remind you that the nuclear button was at one stage at the disposal of a man who might have either pressed it by mistake or else pressed it deliberately in order to obtain room service....

Clive James

An Ego

The ego is by its nature a smallness of being; it brings contraction of the consciousness and with the contraction, limitation of knowledge, disabling ignorance – confinement and a diminution of power, incapacity and weakness – scission of oneness and by that scission, disharmony and failure of sympathy and love and understanding – inhibition or fragmentation of delight of being and by that fragmentation, pain and sorrow. To recover what is lost, we must break out of the worlds of ego.

Aurobindo

An Extremist

A fanatic is one who can't change his mind and won't change the subject.

Winston Churchill

A Friend

Each friend represents a world in us, a world possibly not born until they arrive, and it is only by this meeting that a new world is born.

Anaïs Nin

Hospitality is one form of worship.

The Talmud

An Improviser

He is a great man who accepts the lemons that Fate hands out to him and uses them to start a lemonade-stand.

Elbert Hubbard

An Inventor

The birth of a project is for me like the birth of a little dog or a child. There is a long period of gestation; there is a lot of work in the subconscious before I make the first sketch. That lasts for months. Then one fine morning it takes a form without my knowing it. Each problem provokes in me this interior meditation. I do not depend on my collaborators to solve it. I seek the solution myself, closed up in a room three meters by three meters.

Le Corbusier

A Kindler

The greatest good you can do for another is not just share your riches, but reveal to them their own.

Benjamin Disraeli

In everyone's life, at some time, our inner fire goes out. It is then burst into flame by an encounter with another human being. We should all be thankful for these people who rekindle the inner spirit.

Albert Schweitzer

A Logician

A mind all logic is like a knife all blade. It makes the hand bleed that uses it.

Rabindranath Tagore

A Maverick

The kind of people I look to fill top management spots are the eager beavers, the mavericks. These are the guys who try to do more than they're expected to do – they always reach.

Lee Iacocca

A Mule

Like all weak men, he lay an exaggerated stress on not changing one's mind.

W. Somerset Maugham

A stubborn woman doesn't hold opinions – they hold her.

Adapted from Jacob Braude.

A Relationship Architect

You will never disserve your relationship – nor anyone – by seeing more in another than they are showing you. For there is more there. Much more. It is only their fear that stops them from showing you. If others notice that you see them as more, they will feel safe to show you what you obviously already see.

God, *Conversations with God*, 1, 141

A Revolutionary

Cautious, careful people, always casting about to preserve their reputations… can never effect a reform.

Susan B. Anthony

What is happening in the world is a projection of what is happening inside each one of us; what we are, the world is. Most of us are in turmoil, we are acquisitive, possessive, we are jealous and condemn people; and that is exactly what is happening in the world, only more dramatically, ruthlessly. But neither you nor your teachers spend any time thinking about all this; and it is only when you spend some time every day earnestly thinking about these matters that there is a possibility of bringing about a total revolution and creating a new world. And I assure you, a new world has to be created.

J. Krishnamurti

A Sacrificer

It is impossible to use one relationship at the expense of another and not suffer guilt. And it is equally impossible to condemn part of a relationship and find peace within it.

A Course in Miracles, text, 314

A Salesperson

To succeed in sales, find a way to make your customers successful with your product.

Believe in what you are selling and develop the ability to communicate that belief.

Ray Kroc

A Servant

God loves to see in me, not his servant
But himself who serves all.

Rabindranath Tagore

A Sasquatch

If only the good were a little less heavy-footed!

W. Somerset Maugham

A Skier

Think of life as a ski run, not as a game of chess in which every move is carefully plotted in advance. For there should be a flow in life, a flow that reasoned analysis often only disturbs.

J. Donald Walters

A Truth Sayer

The teacher of truth attracts only those who hunger for the truth.

The URANTIA Book, 1815

A Tyrant

Those who begin coercive elimination of dissent soon find themselves exterminating dissenters. Compulsory unification of opinion achieves only the unanimity of the graveyard.

Felix Frankfurter

Tests

The possession of power is the greatest test of all idealisms.

Aurobindo

WHOSE JOB IS IT?

This is a story about four people named Everybody, Somebody, Anybody, and Nobody. There was an important job to be done and Everybody was asked to do it. Everybody was sure Somebody would do it. Anybody could have done it, but Nobody did it. Somebody got angry about that, because it was Everybody's job. Everybody thought Anybody could to it, but Nobody realized that Everybody wouldn't do it. It ended up that Everybody blamed Somebody when Nobody did what Anybody could have done.

Anonymous

An overall guideline might be this: When in doubt, always err on the side of compassion.

The test of whether you are helping or hurting: Are your fellow humans enlarged or reduced as a result of your help? Have you made them bigger or smaller? More able or less able?

God, Conversations with God, 3, 170

The measure of success is not whether you have a tough problem to deal with, but whether it's the same problem you had last year.

John Foster Dulles

Truth, beauty and goodness stand or fall together. One test of truth therefore is goodness, another is beauty.

N. Sri Ram

Dedications

To Anger

For every minute you are angry you lose sixty seconds of happiness.

Ralph Waldo Emerson

An angry woman is again angry with herself when she returns to reason.

Adapted from Publilius Syrus

Holding onto anger is like grasping a hot coal with the intent of throwing it at someone else; you are the one who gets burned.

Buddha

To Asses

If an ass goes traveling, he'll not come home a horse.

Thomas Fuller

To Attack

If attack thoughts must entail the belief you are vulnerable, their effect is to weaken you in your own eyes. Thus they have attacked your perception of yourself. And because you believe in them, you can no longer believe in yourself. A false image of yourself has come to take the place of what you are.

A Course in Miracles, workbook, 40

To Balance

Ride your emotions as the shallop rides the waves; don't get upset among them. There are people who enjoy getting swamped emotionally, just as, incredibly, there are people who enjoy getting drunk.

Mary Austin

To Beauty

Now, what is beauty? This is one of the most fundamental questions.... To understand what beauty is, to have that sense of goodness which comes when the mind and heart are in communion with something lovely without any hindrance so that one feels completely at ease – surely this has great significance in life; and until we know this response to beauty our lives will be very shallow. One may be surrounded by great beauty, by mountains and fields and rivers, but unless one is alive to it all one might just as well be dead.

J. Krishnamurti

To the Bottom

Do not despise the bottom rungs in the ascent to greatness.

Publilius Syrus

To Calamity

We learn geology the morning after the earthquake.

Ralph Waldo Emerson

If you can keep your head when all about you are losing theirs, it's just possible you haven't grasped the situation.

Jean Kerr

To Choice

We are free up to the point of choice, then the choice controls the chooser.

Mary Crowley

To Commitment

Luis de Leon, returning to his university after five years' imprisonment by the Inquisition, resumed his lectures: "As we were saying yesterday...."

Spanish parable

To Committees

The sound of tireless voices is the price we pay for the right to hear the music of our own opinions.

Adlai Stevenson

To Concentration

The root cause of many failures in life is lack of concentration. Attention is like a searchlight; when its beam is spread over a vast area, its power to focus on a particular object becomes weak, but focused on one thing at a time, it becomes powerful. Great people are people of concentration. They put their whole mind on one thing at a time.

Adapted from Paramahansa Yogananda

To Consistency

Before marriage, a man will lie awake all night thinking about something you said; after marriage, he'll fall asleep before you finish saying it.

Helen Rowland

To Courage

"Come to the edge!"

"No, we cannot, we are afraid."

"Come to the edge!"

"No, we cannot, we'll fall."

"Come to the edge!"

And they came, and he pushed them, and they flew!

Apollinaire

Be brave. The brave alone enjoy the world.

Swami Rama

To Cynics

You may think that the great pity of the cynic is not so much in what he believes as in what he teaches. But they are the same – what he believes, he *does* teach. And he believes fundamentally in hopelessness, helplessness, stupidity and suspicion – and by instilling these thoughts in a child, or anyone who will listen, he teaches a beset, bewildered and false sense of self.

DCJ

To Delicacy

True delicacy, that most beautiful heart-leaf of humanity, exhibits itself most significantly in little things.

Mary Botham Howitt

To Dignity

The only kind of dignity which is genuine is that which is not diminished by the indifference of others.

Dag Hammarskjöld

To Disadvantage

The great pilot can sail even when his canvass is rent.

Seneca

To Disagreement

Other people do not have to change for us to experience peace of mind.

Gerald Jampolsky

To Domination

The Master has no possessions. The more he does for others, the happier he is. The more he gives to others, the wealthier he is. The Tao nourishes by not forcing. By not dominating, the Master leads.

Lao-Tse

To Dullness

Another cause of dullness is imitation. You are made to imitate by tradition. The weight of the past drives you to conform, toe the line, and through conformity the mind feels safe, secure; it establishes itself in a well-oiled groove so that it can run smoothly without disturbance, without a quiver of doubt. Watch the grown-up people about you and you will see that their minds do not want to be disturbed. They want peace, even though it is the peace of death; but real peace is something entirely different.

J. Krishnamurti

To Enslavement

Being incapable of conjugating the verb *to be,* we conjugate the verb *to have.* But as the verb *to have* can lead us nowhere, for nothing lasting can be acquired, we seek indefinitely *to have more.* Such is the source of our enslavement.

Robert Linssen

To Evolution

The highest possible stage in moral culture is when we recognize that we ought to control our thoughts.

Charles Darwin

To Fame

Blessed is he whose fame does not outshine his truth.

Rabindranath Tagore

To Fear

Fear is a stranger to the ways of love. Identify with fear, and you will be a stranger to yourself. And thus you are unknown to you.... Who could be sane in such a circumstance? Who but a madman could believe he is what he is not, and judge against himself?

A Course in Miracles, workbook, 295

Excessive fear is always powerless.

Aeschylus

To Followers

Is there someone who believes in the value of your mission? Ah, I am glad, for without that stimulus you were in a sorry plight. Professor Tyndall once said the finest inspiration he ever received was from an old man who could scarcely read. This man acted as his servant. Each morning the old man would knock on the door of the scientist and call, "Arise, Sir; it is near seven o'clock, and you have great work to do today."

Elbert Hubbard

To Friendliness

There are two kinds of people in the world: those who come into a room and say, "Here I am!" and those who come in and say, "Ah, there you are!"

Anonymous

To Futility

Half our life is spent trying to find something to do with the time we have rushed through life trying to save.

Will Rogers

To Gratitude

No one is as capable of gratitude as one who has emerged from the kingdom of night.

Elie Wiesel

I came to your shore as a stranger, I lived in your house as a guest, I leave your door as a friend, my earth.

Rabindranath Tagore

To Humility

Some people believe there is a great merit and holy virtue in what they think of as humility. Therefore to be proud of oneself seems a sin, and in that frame of reference true affirmation of the self is impossible. Genuine self-pride is the loving recognition of your own integrity and value. True humility is based on this affectionate regard for your self, plus the recognition that you live in a universe in which all other beings also possess this undeniable individuality and self-worth.

Seth

To Incapacity

When you say to me that you can't do this or that, I don't believe it. Whatever you make up your mind to do, you can do. God is the sum total of everything, and His image is within you. He can do anything, and so can you, if you learn to identify yourself with His inexhaustible nature.

Nothing is impossible, unless you think it is.

Paramahansa Yogananda

To Indecisiveness

I don't like to commit myself about heaven and hell – you see, I have friends in both places.

Mark Twain

To the Inner Voice

And thanks to you for listening to Him. His Word is soundless if it be not heard. In thanking Him the thanks are yours as well. An unheard message will not save the world, however mighty be the Voice that speaks, however loving may the message be.

A Course in Miracles, workbook, 216

To Justice

The passing of an unjust law is the suicide of authority.

Pastoral letter

To Mistakes

Every great mistake has a halfway moment, a split second when it can be recalled and perhaps remedied.

Pearl S. Buck

To Over-anxiousness

To undertake to supply people with a thing you think they need, but which they do not want, is to have your head elevated on a pike, and your bones buried in the Potter's Field. But wait, and the world will yet want the thing it needs, and your bones may then become sacred relics.

Elbert Hubbard

To Perfection

When nobody around you seems to measure up, it's time to check your yardstick.

Bill Lemley

The perfect round of golf has never been played. It's eighteen holes-in-one. I almost dreamt it once, but I lipped out at eighteen.

Ben Hogan

To the Plan

In the beginning there was THE PLAN.

And then came the ASSUMPTIONS,

And the assumptions were without form,

And the PLAN was completely without substance,

And darkness was upon the face of the EMPLOYEES,

And they spoke among themselves, saying,

"It is a crock of shit and it stinks."

And the employees went unto their supervisors, saying,

"It is a pail of dung and none may abide the odor thereof."

And the supervisors went unto the managers, saying,

"It is a container of excrement and it is very strong such that none may abide by it."

And the managers went unto their directors, saying,

"It is a vessel of fertilizer and none may abide its strength."

And the directors went unto their executive directors saying,

"It contains that which aids plant growth and is very strong."

And the executive directors went unto the general manager, saying,

"It promotes growth and is powerful."

And the general manager went unto the board of directors, saying,

"This new plan will actively promote the growth and efficiency of this organization and these areas in particular."

And the board of directors looked upon the plan and saw that it was good,

And the plan became policy.

This is how shit happens.

Anonymous

To Prejudice

Ordinary people think that the joy or pain which they get from being with people whom they like or dislike, comes from those people; but it is not so. It is one's own likes and dislikes which are responsible for one's joy or sorrow.

Sathya Sai Baba

To Pride

People often oppose a thing merely because they have no agency in planning it, or because it may have been planned by those whom they dislike.

Adapted from Alexander Hamilton

Your pride will cause you total ruin.

Sathya Sai Baba

To Renunciation

If you resolve to give up smoking, drinking and loving, you don't actually live longer; it just seems longer.

Clement Freud

To Revenge

Those who seek revenge should dig two graves.

Chinese proverb

To Rules

Precedents, procedures, rules and regulations I have aplenty, but my oldest friends, I realized one troubling day, are kindness and compassion. And these friends must stand first, before all else.

DCJ

To Sincerity

"Sincerity is everything!" Yogananda said to his teacher.

"No," responded Yukteswar, "sincerity plus thoughtfulness is everything."

To Truth

Be open to the truth, no matter who is speaking it. If you smell smoke, and a parrot squawks, "The house is on fire!" is that the moment to reassure others, "Oh, but the parrot doesn't understand what it's saying"?

J. Donald Walters

Truth is a river that is always splitting up into arms that reunite. Islanded between the arms, the inhabitants argue for a lifetime as to which is the main river.

Cyril Connolly

To Uncertainty

When a man does not know what harbor he is making for, no wind is the right wind.

Seneca

To the Untrustworthy

When people are convinced that the self is untrustworthy, for whatever reasons, or that the universe is not safe, then instead of luxuriating in the use of their abilities, exploring the physical and mental environments, they begin to pull in their realities – to contract their abilities, to overcontrol their environments. They become frightened people – and frightened people do not want freedom, mental or physical. They want shelter, a definite set of rules. They want to be told what is good and bad. They lean toward compulsive behavior patterns. They seek out leaders – political, scientific, or religious – who will order their lives for them.

Seth

To Useless Leaders

A leader is useless when he acts against the promptings of his own conscience.

Mahatma Gandhi

To Violent Leaders

The source of violence is the "me," the ego, the self, which expresses itself in so many ways – in division, in trying to become or be somebody – which divides itself as the "me" and the "not me," as the unconscious and the conscious; the "me" that identifies with the family or not with the family, with the community or not with the community and so on. It is like a stone dropped in a lake: the waves spread and spread, at the center is the "me." As long as the "me" survives in any form, very subtly or grossly, there must be violence.

J. Krishnamurti

To You

What you have become is the price you paid to get what you used to want.

Mignon McLaughlin

Small Mercies

Procrastination gives you something to look forward to.

Joan Konner

Tyranny is always better organized than freedom.

Charles-Pierre Péguy

By working faithfully eight hours a day, you may eventually get to be boss and work twelve hours a day.

Robert Frost

Money is never so well spent as when you get cheated out of it – for at one stroke you have purchased prudence.

Arthur Schopenhauer

When you're in love, it's the most glorious two-and-a-half days of your life.

Richard Lewis

The Aging Leader

In his old age, Churchill overheard a new MP whisper to another – "They say the old man's getting a bit past it."

Said Churchill, "And they say the old man's getting deaf as well."

You should retire only when you can find something you enjoy doing more than what you are doing now.

George Burns

Flow with life's changes. Don't get trapped in an abandoned time frame. The secret of aging gracefully is to greet every new experience with a fresh, creative outlook.

J. Donald Walters

As you grow older in years and more experienced in the affairs of the kingdom, are you becoming more tactful in dealing with troublesome mortals and more tolerant in living with stubborn subordinates? Tact is the fulcrum of social leverage, and tolerance is the earmark of a great soul. If you possess these rare and charming gifts, as the days pass you will become more alert and expert in your worthy efforts to avoid all unnecessary social misunderstandings. Such wise souls are able to avoid much of the trouble which is certain to be the portion of all who suffer from lack of emotional adjustment, those who refuse to grow up, and those who refuse to grow old gracefully.

The URANTIA Book, 1740

Epilog

One more good soul on earth is better than an extra angel in heaven.

Chinese proverb

The idea of enlightenment is of utmost importance. Just to know that there is such a possibility, changes one's entire outlook. It acts like a burning match in a heap of sawdust.... A spark of truth can burn up a mountain of lies.... All great teachers did nothing else.

Nisargadatta Maharaj

Every moment and every event of our life on earth plants something in our soul. For just as the wind carries thousands of winged seeds, so each moment brings with it germs of spiritual vitality that come to rest imperceptibly in the minds and wills of people. Most of these unnumbered seeds perish and are lost, because we are not prepared to receive them; for such seeds as these cannot spring up anywhere except in the good soil of freedom, spontaneity and love.

Adapted from Thomas Merton

As you grow older you will find that your desires are never really fulfilled. In fulfillment there is always the shadow of frustration, and in your heart there is not a song but a cry. The desire to become – to become a great man, a great saint, a great this or that – has no end and therefore no fulfillment; its demand is ever for the "more," and such desire always breeds agony, misery, wars. But when one is free of all desire to become, there is a state of being whose action is totally different. It is. That which is has no time. It does not think in terms of fulfillment. Its very being is its fulfillment.

J. Krishnamurti

There is a way of living so vitally, freshly, originally, spontaneously and dynamically that life becomes a transformation, a state of perpetual joy, a native ecstasy which nothing can take away.

N. Sri Ram

When I despair, I remember that all through history the way of truth and love has always won. There have been tyrants and murderers, and for a time they seem invincible, but in the end they always fall – think of it, always.

Mahatma Gandhi

Realize your uniqueness in the entire universe. No one will ever have your song to sing: Through all eternity it is yours alone. Your primary task in life is to learn that song, and to sing it perfectly.

J. Donald Walters

Our right and natural road is towards the summits.

Aurobindo